Presentation by *BookLeaf Publishing*

Web: www.bookleafpub.com

E-mail: info@bookleafpub.com

ISBN: 9789360946487

First edition 2024

For Larry Fountain. The love of my life, my twin flame, the man who makes me crazy. I wouldn't write poems if you didn't piss me off. Please never stop. I'll love you forever.

And my 3 kids. Akira, Billy and Freya Fountain. Who are actually cats but still my children.

ACKNOWLEDGEMENT

I have a few thank you's I'd like to say! Thank you to Book Leaf Publishing for making my dream come true. A published Poet, can you believe it!? Using Book Leaf Publishing made this a breeze and stress free. Thank you to my best friend, Jessica, of 20 years. Through tweendom to adult, you encouraged me to create. Together as girls we navigated the horrors of adolescence and learned to channel our pain into art. Thank you for sticking around through all of life's ups and downs and never ever turning your back on me. Thank you for reading everything I send you and giving me your honest reviews. Thank you in advance for the friendship and sisterhood you'll give me until we're 97 years old, wheelchair racing down the hallway in the nursing home. Thank you to my mom, Heather, for being everything to me. In case you couldn't tell, I'm a bit obsessed with my mom. For good reason though. She never lets me down. She's made a life time commitment to take care of her children and to her there is no age limit on that. As I age, she only shows me more support. My mother is not a big fan of poetry but she has made it known she supports me and believes in me every step of the way. Thank you for being my best friend and correcting all my spelling mistakes. My final thank you goes to my fiancé, Larry. Thank you, my love, for being a good sport and supporting me even though the majority of my poems are about him and not in the best light. Thank you for understanding that what I write isn't a reflection of who you are or what you do but a reflection of me and how I perceive and react to situations. You are the only person who can take on my moods and turn them around. Thank you for taking care of me financially so I have the freedom and time to create. Thank you for sparking my idea of publishing my work so many years ago and for encouraging me to do it every time I backed down. You are the love of my life, my biggest pain and my greatest muse. Sometimes I can't believe this is real. Thank you, Larry, for staying.

The Greatest Gift

I dug a pit of despair and called it home
I lived every second in fight or flight
When my shadow was frightening
As a clown lurking in the sewers
I fell victim to my formidable mind
One hundred different masks to hide myself
To keep the crazy locked away
A handful of pills just to make me smile
I couldn't stand the sight of a mirror

Then he asked me to be his eternally
And something in me changed
Where there were violent stormy skies
Now beams of light show radiant color
That I was missing for so long
But instead of obsessing over him
I finally became the star of my life
Learning about my brain
So I can be to the best of my ability

I find myself winking at my reflection
Taking one hundred selfies a day
Feeling good enough in my skin
For the first time in my life
I catch myself dancing

Without a care in the world
Lyrically narrating everything we do
And its okay that I'm weird because
You've given me the greatest gift
A safe place to be my wild and silly
And sometimes unhinged self

Mother

My mother is the kindest soul
She would do anything for anyone
She's someone who goes with the flow
You'd never know when she's upset
She is too proud to show her tears
My mother deserves a better life
And it pains me I can't give that to her
She has given me everything I ask for
And I treat her poorly sometimes
I'm short tempered and mentally ill
but she accepts me wholly in any mood
I hope my mother knows
That she is the only person
I feel completely comfortable around
And that is the only reason
That I lose control when she's here
It physically pains me when I yell
And I see her smile fade
I work so hard to keep in line
Because I love my mom more than life
I wish I would never hurt her
But I thank god every day
For giving me a mother who accepts me
And has learned to navigate my shifts
I pray she knows what she means to me

And I hope I fill her heart up
With so much joy and love
That she doesn't take it personally
When I am being mean
My mother deserves better from the world
And much better from me

Softie

On the outside he's strong and ridged
with a don't fuck with me attitude
He's quick to anger and ready to shout
A bad boy I just can't live without

His affection is few and far between
So it always shocks me when I feel his touch
The soft and tenderness that he gives out
Is proof of his love that I cannot doubt

When he kisses me my world spins
His gentle tongue makes my heart stop
The solid confirmation that this love is true
I found my mate my soul already knew

Sometimes I wish I would receive more
A cuddle here, a kiss goodbye there
Compliments and tight hugs when I'm sad
I often wish he'd just hold my hand

But he shows me he loves me in other ways
I have learned and accepted over the years
I don't need physical affection all the time
To feel so thankful and lucky that he's mine

Mutual Obsession

I can't make anyone love me
Or want to spend time with me
I'm not sure what I do
To make others go the other way
I am too much or not enough
And I wish I could let it go
Let them walk away
Without the pain I feel inside
I wish I didn't need anyone else
To enjoy the life I'm living
But I hate to be alone
And I need actions to prove your love
I can't stand small talk
But engaging conversations
Just don't happen anymore
Maybe I'm not worth the effort
Or they can't find the time
I hate that I'd do anything
For anyone I love
But I spend my days alone
In deafening silence
My only saving grace
Is a man obsessed with me
Needing my presence
As much as I need his

Maybe my little family
Is all that I really need
To feel the happiness within me

Toxicity

Going from the toxic couple
To the ones stable and together
Really is a beautiful thing
When you expect an explosion
But get a shrug instead
A peacefulness sets in
But even still I feel something missing

In our hate fueled angry haze
Spewing poison at one another
It might have seemed the love was gone
But what kept us going
Kept us at each others throats
Was fire burning passion
You can't hate someone
If you don't love them

I miss our passion
I miss your jealousy
I miss the desire in your eyes
No one talks about the addiction
Toxicity creates
Or the heart breaking withdrawal
From the passion filled arguments
That led to ravenous desire

YOU

I wish you could see yourself
Through my eyes for just a day
At the end you'd have no insecurities
Never having to wonder again
You'd see the way my heart takes off
When my hands find you in the bed
Knowing you're next to me
Starts and ends my days with peace

Everything I do has to do with you
My only goal being your happiness
There's no length I wouldn't go
To see a smile on your face or
To hear your laughter in the air
You are a master piece to admire
And I will never grow tired of the view

You are my best friend and lover too
The man I dreamed of when I was a child
Your presence I crave at all times
My only safe place is in your arms
And I swear your skin is magical too
One tiny touch from you and I come alive
Healing broken pieces of me so
I can be wholly healthy me just for you

I have loved you for so long
It will never fade away
Grow old with me my honey
And make life exactly as I wanted
Fully consumed in love
Living happily ever after
With one another forever

A Place To Be Me

I sometimes forget, as that happens so naturally for me, to keep my mask secured snuggly to my face. When I feel comfortable and safe a sliver of ME might peak out. Instant regret fills the space between my bones, embarrassment painting my face. I glance at him holding my breathe, waiting for the shame to deepen. I see the reflection, music to my ears. A silent acceptance laced with love. An open invitation for a place to let down my walls and breathe. This is the greatest gift he's given me.

Storm Clouds

They used to fill me with anxiety
The loud thunder and crashing
Of lighting
But as I age I find myself
On the porch in search of
Peace
The angry sky so much
Like the my cloudy mind
Storms roll in and
Scream and shout
Sometimes leaving destruction
In its path
But you forgive because that's
Just nature
So forgive me too
When the weight is too much
And I let it rain
And rumble through the night
For it's just human nature to
Let it all out

Thank You

Sometimes when the clouds clear
And the sun or moon are bright
The grass is lush and green
I can take a big deep breath
And see clearly what's in front of me

I am enormously grateful
For the life that I live
For the man that I love
Who provides me with this home
A beautiful place that I made
Where we shut the world out
And enjoy each other and our solitude

He doesn't hold it over my head
All the things I have thanks to him
But it's the truth that I over look
That I take for granted every day
I provide us a lot too
But I owe this charming life
Mostly to you and all the work you do

It's not enough but
Thank you for giving me
A home to lay my head

A heart to fill with love
My girls to give me purpose
And the space to be myself
Thank you for this life
That I've always dreamed about

No Passion

There is no passion
No uncontrolled laughing
Or tears of joy
There is no excitement
Or fun times to share
No compliments given
To uplift my soul

All that's left is me
Inside my head
Wondering why
You don't love me
Anymore

A Sense Of Impending Doom

Heart racing
Oh no oh no oh no
My pulse hammers in my ear drums
Oh god something bad
Something really really bad
It's coming and nothing can stop it
Breathless and clammy
With shaking hands
I pick at my nails
My mind is reeling
How can this be happening
And how can I prepare
For the pain it will cause
I don't know what is coming
I just know it's close
Something really bad is very near
And I am starting to panic

Breathe in and out
In and out again and again
What can you see
What can you hear
What can you taste
What can you feel
What can you smell

You are safe now
Nothing is coming
Nothing is near

Poor sweet Shwade
Her mind got the best of her
Again

I Am So Sorry

I am so sorry that I took your voice away
I wasn't strong enough back then
I'm sorry that I wasn't brave
Creating a personal hell just for you
I'm sorry that you missed out
On a childhood filled with wonder
I'm sorry that you lived your life
Terrified of any kind of rejection
Please forgive me for the years
I've neglected you and your pain
I want you to know that it's not your fault
Family swept the skeletons under the rug
He became the prestige and it wasn't fair
But that's no reflection on you dear
You did the best you could do
With the shitty hand that was dealt
It's not your fault, sweet little girl
It's not your burden to carry alone
I am here now and I'll never leave
You didn't feel love back then
And yet still we really don't
But now that we're together
I'll love you enough
To wash away the demons
That's been holding us under

Please forgive me my inner child
Forgive me for being too young
And too alone and too scared
Forgive me for years of silence
For accepting the abuse
You never ever deserved
Forgive me for forgiving them
Without any resolution
Forgive me for not healing
The deep scars within
Please forgive me and I promise
To never let you go to sleep crying
All alone encased in darkness again
Look around and you will see
I'm right here holding your hand
For every hug and kiss
Every I'm proud of you
And I love you that you missed
I'll fill you up with all the tenderness
That you were often denied
Together we'll get through this
 Healing this broken tattered heart
Collectively we will feel love again
Like we did before your innocence
Was so cruelly stolen away

A Silent War

At 3am when all is quiet
You're sleeping soundly
And I should be too
Yet I can't help but stare
At the peace on your face
For I know you're taking a break
From a silent war that rages on
Inside that intricate mind

Proud

Is it really so few and far between
When I am an actual functioning adult
That you'd need to point it out
And tell me that you're so proud

When everything aligns
I am what you want
A few weeks of normality
Suppress the crazy
And now you love me

Don't get me wrong
Praise and a kiss are special
And I feel proud too

But I'd give up anything
Anything at all
For you to love me
All the time
And to make you proud
In some small way
Everyday

What Have I Done?

It must be the gaps in my memory
Buried in there so deep
That I can't find a hint of it

Something so cruel and evil
A disturbing crime committed by me

I had to of done something bad
To deserve all this pain
It seems I'm most deserving
For this game you want to play

Turn off your love for me
I guess I can handle that
But do you need to hurt me
And make my skin crawl
When I'm in your presence too

Gaslighting and accusations
Defensive comebacks and sneers
Quiet phones and empty hearts
a broken family we've become

I try to do all things in kindness
I'd never intentionally hurt you

You said I deserved all the love
So please tell me now
What have I done

Destination: We Made It

We're pretty far down the road
Even with carrying this load
Obstacles tried to slow us down
But like our hands, we know this town

Life turned dark and dreary
Causing us to become weary
Stress and anxiety filled us up
Morphing into violent blowups

Words like daggers leaving scars
Fill my lungs with smoke to see stars
A miserable life led by jealousy
Holding onto each other desperately

A day filled with love ended in despair
Two lovers against each other wasn't fair
Fighting for our lives against destiny
Only causing a painful penalty

250 days apart felt like I was dying
I was given the strength to keep trying
I worked on myself and hoped you did the same
Scanning social media for a glimpse of your
name

You burst through all of my protections
Said you couldn't deny our connections
8 months of silence was long enough
Life without you was way too rough

Reunited and working towards a goal
The past behind us left in the hole
We climbed out together into the sun
Hand in hand we merged into one

Violence destroyed by communication
We saved our love from damnation
We grow stronger with synchronicity
And strip ourselves of our toxicity

While we're in a great place right now
Staying sedentary we have to disavow
If we keep it going steady and strong
We can get there before too long

Our destination is coming into sight
The road there illuminated by moonlight
A simple but happy life ready to commit
When we can finally say "we made it"

Shattered

So we're back to this place
Where a ding from a phone
Puts my body in a panic
The racing thoughts ran rampid
With what I've done or haven't
To deserve the pain you're causing

Broken promises rain down
And scatter on the floor
Remnants of trust laying all around me
Mocking me for ever believing
That this could be all mine
My perfect happily ever after

My hopes
My dreams
My happiness
My trust
My heart
SHATTERED

Hold Me Close

I am not crazy or insane
I am simply a woman
Who has mental illness
And a learning disability
I do not understand
Why you call me names
Or insist I'm irresponsible
My brain does not work
The same as yours
I deserve a little grace
After what I've been through
I beat myself up enough
Day in and day out
For failing at the simple things
I really don't think
That I need help
Putting me down

I really need a hug
When everything goes wrong
When I forget what I'm doing
When I can't remember
Anything I need to
When cleaning is too much
And a shower feels exhausting

When it's too loud
Or too crowded
I know you get frustrated
But I don't do it on purpose
I don't want to cry
I just want to be held
I want to feel safe
Inside of your arms
Not afraid of words
Coming from your mouth

Daydreaming

How long can someone live without love?
Will my heart dry out and begin to crack
Will the remnants of my happiness
Leak out as tears from my eyes?
My kindness and compassion evaporated
Leaving bitterness and resentment?
How do I live without hugs and kisses
Without fingers intertwined with mine?
How do I keep going without warmth?
A body pressing against me is foreign
And I've never known how to cuddle
Daydreams of intimacy fill my time
Consumed by desire and longing
I ache to be in strong arms
Wrapped up all around me
With a pressure so secure
It heals my broken heart
It feels so good when I love on him
And I imagine it's better to be loved
But Maybe I'll never know the feeling
Please breathe love into me
And stop this insufferable desolation

Momma

She is the vibrant yellow
You see up in the sky
She is the calm
During the endless storms
She is the voice of reason
When nothing makes sense
She is the comedian
When it's hard to smile
She is the warm embrace
When I feel all alone
She is the undying strength
When I want to give up
She is the fan club
When everyone left
She is all the love
I someday want to feel

She doesn't know
What she means
To my heart
Maybe she never will.
But when our times come
Bury us together because
I never want to be apart

Childhood Trauma

I barely slept at all
But it's always been that way
It's 4am and he's already yelling
I get out of bed and hope that
The coffee will jolt me alive
I take my Adderall and
Give it the ole "please work"
I spend 30 minutes reading
Self-help to improve me
I go get dressed and
Pick up my messy room
A long drive with
Heavy eye lids
It's a struggle every day
Work goes quick but
I'm pretty exhausted
Overstimulation wears you out
I rush home to be with him
But he ignores me once again
I want to sit but he wants dinner
Two hours and a huge mess later
Now he wants the kitchen cleaned
And why is the bathroom so dirty
And dont forget to take a shower too
I forgot to turn the light off

He gets so upset with me
It's 9pm and I can finally
Get off of my aching feet
And go to my comfy bed
To barely sleep and
Do it all over again and again.
He really wants to know
Why can't I just be an adult?
Im not an expert but I think
Because I cannot heal
When I am still surrounded
By my childhood trauma